TAPAS

TAPAS

EASY RECIPES FOR TASTY TAPAS DISHES

written by Susanna Tee

Parragon Publishing
Queen Street House
4 Queen Street
Bath BA1 1HE, UK

ISBN: 978-1-4075-3956-0

Printed in China

Cover design by Andrew Easton at UMMAGUMMA
Internal design by Fiona Roberts
Produced by the Bridgewater Book Company Ltd
Photography by David Jordan
Home economy by Jacqueline Bellefontaine

Notes for the Reader

This book uses imperial, metric, or US cup measurements. Follow the same units of
measurement throughout; do not mix imperial and metric. All spoon measurements are
level: teaspoons are assumed to be 5 ml, and tablespoons are assumed to be 15 ml.
Unless otherwise stated, milk is assumed to be whole, eggs and individual vegetables
such as potatoes are medium, and pepper is freshly ground black pepper. Recipes using
raw or very lightly cooked eggs should be avoided by infants, the elderly, pregnant women,
convalescents, and anyone suffering from an illness.

Picture acknowledgment

The Bridgewater Book Company would like to thank Owen Franken/Corbis for permission
to reproduce copyright material for the endpapers.

Introduction

SMALL, IRRESISTIBLE MOUTHFULS OF SOMETHING SAVORY, SERVED WITH A CHILLED WHITE WINE, BEER, OR SHERRY—THESE ARE TAPAS, THE NATIONAL INSTITUTION OF SPAIN, EATEN WITH ENTHUSIASM IN ALMOST EVERY BAR BEFORE LUNCH AND DINNER.

The word tapa actually means lid, and comes from the slices of bread that the innkeeper would place on top of a person's wine glass to keep out the flies and dust between sips. The Andalucians then thought of the idea of balancing some kind of small food on top of this piece of bread, and tapas were born.

A full array of these tasty miniature morsels can make an informal lunch or dinner in themselves. For a meal, serve six to eight dishes, making your choice from a couple of recipes in each chapter. In addition, serve a selection of simple dishes, such as bowls of large olives and salted almonds, and accompany these with a selection of salads.

Whatever your choice of recipes, tapas are for sharing and lingering over with a glass of something chilled. Eating tapas goes hand-in-hand with hospitality, friendship, and lots of great conversation. Enjoy the experience!

Just one bite means exactly that! Almost all tapas are no more than a mouthful, but the recipes in this chapter really are literally only that. It makes them the perfect partner to serve with pre-dinner drinks or at a drinks party, particularly as they are easy to pick up with your fingers. Highly flavored and small, these appetizers whet your appetite but leave room for something else.

The simplest tapas dishes include a few slices of serrano ham or spicy chorizo sausage, a bowl of olives, cubes of manchego cheese, olive oil-soaked garlic bread, artichoke hearts, pan-fried shrimp, anchovies, or salted almonds. These are the original tapas dishes that were offered along with a drink before they became more elaborate in a bid to attract customers. Recipes are hardly needed for some of these dishes, but this book gives you ideas for what to serve along with more substantial recipes.

JUST ONE BITE

Do provide toothpicks to spear these small delicacies and a saucer on which to discard the empty sticks! In some bars, the tapas are served on toothpicks and are known as *pinchos*. These all cost the same amount and, before a customer leaves, the waiter will count up the number of empty toothpicks to add to the bill. It is an inexpensive and enjoyable way of eating out.

SERVES 8 AS PART
OF A TAPAS MEAL
1 lb/450 g can or jar unpitted
  large green olives, drained
4 garlic cloves, peeled
2 tsp coriander seeds

1 small lemon
4 sprigs of fresh thyme
4 feathery stalks of fennel
2 small fresh red chilies (optional)
pepper
Spanish extra virgin olive oil, to cover

Cracked Marinated Olives

The olives will keep in the refrigerator for several months, and in fact the longer you marinate them, the more their flavor will be enhanced. Use the oil that they have been marinated in either for cooking or in a salad dressing. It will impart a delicious flavor to a dish.

• To allow the flavors of the marinade to penetrate the olives, place on a cutting board and, using a rolling pin, bash them lightly so that they crack slightly. Alternatively, use a sharp knife to cut a lengthwise slit in each olive as far as the pit. Using the flat side of a broad knife, lightly crush each garlic clove. Using a mortar and pestle, crack the coriander seeds. Cut the lemon, with its rind, into small chunks.

• Put the olives, garlic, coriander seeds, lemon chunks, thyme sprigs, fennel, and chilies, if using, in a large bowl and toss together. Season with pepper to taste, but you should not need to add salt as preserved olives are usually salty enough. Pack the ingredients tightly into a glass jar with a lid. Pour in enough olive oil to cover the olives, then seal the jar tightly.

• Let the olives stand at room temperature for 24 hours, then marinate in the refrigerator for at least 1 week but preferably 2 weeks before serving. From time to time, gently give the jar a shake to remix the ingredients. Return the olives to room temperature and remove from the oil to serve. Provide toothpicks for spearing the olives.

SERVES 6–8 AS PART
OF A TAPAS MEAL

scant 1½ cups whole almonds,
 in their skins or blanched
 (see method)

4 tbsp Spanish olive oil

coarse sea salt

1 tsp paprika or ground cumin
 (optional)

Salted Almonds

Almonds are the most popular nut to be salted and served as a tapa in Spain, but hazelnuts are also popular and can be prepared in exactly the same way. Walnut halves, pistachios, peanuts, and cashews could also be given the same treatment.

• Preheat the oven to 350°F/180°C. Fresh almonds in their skins are superior in taste, but blanched almonds are much more convenient. If the almonds are not blanched, put them in a bowl, cover with boiling water for 3–4 minutes, then plunge them into cold water for 1 minute. Drain them well in a strainer, then slide off the skins between your fingers. Dry the almonds well on paper towels.

• Put the olive oil in a roasting pan and swirl it round so that it covers the bottom. Add the almonds and toss them in the pan so that they are evenly coated in the oil, then spread them out in a single layer.

• Roast the almonds in the oven for 20 minutes, or until they are light golden brown, tossing several times during the cooking. Drain the almonds on paper towels, then transfer them to a bowl.

• While the almonds are still warm, sprinkle with plenty of sea salt and the paprika or cumin, if using, and toss well together to coat. Serve the almonds warm or cold. The almonds are at their best when served freshly cooked, so, if possible, cook them on the day that you plan to eat them. However, they can be stored in an airtight container for up to 3 days.

SERVES 6 AS PART
OF A TAPAS MEAL
1 lb/450 g white mushrooms
5 tbsp Spanish olive oil
2 garlic cloves, finely chopped

squeeze of lemon juice
salt and pepper
4 tbsp chopped fresh flatleaf parsley
crusty bread, to serve

Sautéed Garlic Mushrooms

Wild mushrooms such as boletuses or chanterelles can be used in place of cultivated mushrooms. Zucchini may also be prepared in the same way, with a chopped small onion cooked in the oil until lightly browned before adding the garlic.

• Wipe or brush clean the mushrooms, then trim off the stalks close to the caps. Cut any large mushrooms in half or into quarters. Heat the olive oil in a large, heavy-bottom skillet, add the garlic and cook for 30 seconds–1 minute, or until lightly browned. Add the mushrooms and sauté over high heat, stirring most of the time, until the mushrooms have absorbed all the oil in the skillet.

• Reduce the heat to low. When the juices have come out of the mushrooms, increase the heat again, and sauté for 4–5 minutes, stirring most of the time, until the juices have almost evaporated. Add a squeeze of lemon juice and season to taste with salt and pepper. Stir in the parsley and cook for an additional minute.

• Transfer the sautéed mushrooms to a warmed serving dish and serve piping hot or warm. Accompany with chunks or slices of crusty bread for mopping up the garlic cooking juices.

SERVES 8 AS PART
OF A TAPAS MEAL
24 cherry tomatoes

ANCHOVY AND OLIVE FILLING
1¾ oz/50 g canned anchovies in
    olive oil
8 pimiento-stuffed green olives,
    finely chopped

2 large hard-cooked eggs,
    finely chopped
pepper

OR CRAB SALAD FILLING
6 oz/175 g canned crabmeat, drained
4 tbsp mayonnaise
1 tbsp chopped fresh flatleaf parsley
salt and pepper

OR BLACK OLIVE AND
CAPER FILLING
12 pitted black olives
3 tbsp capers
6 tbsp Aïoli (see page 92)
salt and pepper

Stuffed Cherry Tomatoes

Cherry tomatoes are made for just one mouthful but, if you prefer, larger tomatoes could be stuffed with the fillings. The quantities given in the recipe will fill about 10 medium tomatoes.

• Several different choices of filling have been given in this recipe, so make a decision before you start, or, of course, you could make a selection of each. Simply cut the filling quantities to stuff the corresponding number of tomatoes. If necessary, cut and discard a very thin slice from the stalk end of each tomato to make the bases flat and stable.
• Cut a thin slice from the smooth end of each tomato and discard. Using a serrated knife or teaspoon, loosen the pulp and seeds of each and scoop out, discarding the flesh. Turn the scooped-out tomatoes upside down on paper towels and let drain for 5 minutes.
• To make the Anchovy and Olive Filling, drain the anchovies, reserving the oil for later, chop finely, and put in a bowl. Add the olives and hard-cooked eggs. Pour in a trickle of oil from the drained anchovies to moisten the mixture, season with pepper (don't add salt to season as the anchovies will provide enough) and mix well together.
• To make the Crab Salad Filling, put the crabmeat, mayonnaise, and parsley in a bowl and mix well together. Season the filling to taste with salt and pepper.
• To make the Black Olive and Caper Filling, put the olives and capers on paper towels to drain them well, then chop finely and put in a bowl. Add the Aïoli and mix well together. Season the filling to taste with salt and pepper.
• Fill a pastry bag fitted with a ¾-inch/2-cm plain tip with the filling of your choice and use to pack the filling into the hollow tomato shells. Store the tomatoes in the refrigerator until ready to serve.

SERVES 6–8 AS PART
OF A TAPAS MEAL
7 oz/200 g chorizo sausage,
   outer casing removed
4 thick slices 2-day-old country bread

Spanish olive oil, for pan-frying
3 garlic cloves, finely chopped
2 tbsp chopped fresh flatleaf parsley
paprika, to garnish

Garlic Pan-Fried Bread and Chorizo

Choose a soft chorizo sausage for this recipe as, although it will not have been cured for a long period, the soft varieties usually contain a high proportion of fat, which makes them very good for cooking. As an alternative to chorizo, you could use thickly cut serrano ham or even garlic sausage.

• Cut the chorizo sausage into $1/2$-inch/1-cm thick slices and cut the bread, with its crusts still on, into $1/2$-inch/1-cm cubes. Add enough olive oil to a large, heavy-bottom skillet so that it generously covers the bottom. Heat the oil, add the garlic, and cook for 30 seconds–1 minute, or until lightly browned.

• Add the bread cubes to the skillet and pan-fry, stirring all the time, until golden brown and crisp. Add the chorizo slices and pan-fry for 1–2 minutes, or until hot. Using a slotted spoon, remove the bread cubes and chorizo from the skillet and drain well on paper towels.

• Turn the pan-fried bread and chorizo into a warmed serving bowl, add the chopped parsley, and toss together. Garnish the dish with a sprinkling of paprika and serve warm. Accompany with toothpicks so that a piece of sausage and a cube of bread can be speared together for eating.

SERVES 8 AS PART
OF A TAPAS MEAL
12 small globe artichokes
juice of ½ lemon
2 tbsp Spanish olive oil
1 small orange-fleshed melon,
  such as cantaloupe

7 oz/200 g chorizo sausage,
  outer casing removed
few sprigs of fresh tarragon
  or flatleaf parsley, to garnish

DRESSING
3 tbsp Spanish extra virgin olive oil
1 tbsp red wine vinegar
1 tsp prepared mustard
1 tbsp chopped fresh tarragon
salt and pepper

A Salad of Melon, Chorizo, and Artichokes

If you are unable to find fresh artichokes, you could use 14 oz/400 g canned artichoke hearts. Simply drain the juices from the can and slice the artichoke hearts in half or in quarters. As a variation, you could use serrano ham, cut in one thick piece rather than sliced, instead of the chorizo.

• To prepare the artichokes, cut off the stalks, then break off the toughest outer leaves at the base until the tender inside leaves are visible. Using a pair of scissors, cut the spiky tips off the leaves. Using a sharp knife, pare the dark green skin from the base and down the stem. As you prepare them, brush the cut surfaces of the artichokes with lemon juice to prevent discoloration. Alternatively, fill a bowl with cold water to which you have added a little lemon juice, and immerse the artichokes in the acidulated water to stop discoloration. Carefully remove the choke (the mass of silky hairs) by pulling it out with your fingers or by scooping it out with a spoon. It is very important to remove all the choke as the little barbs, if eaten, can irritate the throat. However, if you are using very young artichokes, you do not need to worry about removing the choke and you can include the stalk too, well scraped, as it will be quite tender. Cut the artichokes into quarters and brush them again with lemon juice.
• Heat the olive oil in a large, heavy-bottom skillet, then add the prepared artichokes and cook, stirring frequently, for 5 minutes, or until the artichoke leaves are golden brown. Remove from the skillet, transfer to a large serving bowl, and let cool.
• To prepare the melon, cut in half and scoop out the seeds with a spoon. Cut the flesh into bite-size cubes. Add to the cooled artichokes. Cut the chorizo into bite-size chunks and add to the melon and artichokes.
• To make the dressing, put all the ingredients in a bowl and whisk together. Just before serving, pour the dressing over the prepared salad ingredients and toss together. Serve the salad garnished with tarragon or parsley sprigs.

SERVES 6–8 AS PART
OF A TAPAS MEAL
2 large eggplants
2 red bell peppers
4 tbsp Spanish olive oil
2 garlic cloves, coarsely chopped

grated rind and juice of ½ lemon
1 tbsp chopped fresh cilantro,
    plus extra sprigs to garnish
½–1 tsp paprika
salt and pepper
bread or toast, to serve

Eggplant and Bell Pepper Dip

Instead of cooking the eggplants and bell peppers in the oven, they can be cooked under the broiler until the skins are charred all over. They do, however, need to be turned frequently and they will take about 10 minutes. This dip is also very good served with cold meats.

• Preheat the oven to 375°F/190°C. Prick the skins of the eggplants and bell peppers all over with a fork and brush with about 1 tablespoon of the olive oil. Put on a baking sheet and bake in the oven for 45 minutes, or until the skins are starting to turn black, the flesh of the eggplant is very soft, and the bell peppers are deflated.

• When the vegetables are cooked, put them in a bowl and immediately cover tightly with a clean, damp dish towel. Alternatively, you can put the vegetables in a plastic bag. Let them stand for about 15 minutes, until they are cool enough to handle.

• When the vegetables have cooled, cut the eggplants in half lengthwise, carefully scoop out the flesh, and discard the skin. Cut the eggplant flesh into large chunks. Remove and discard the stem, core, and seeds from the bell peppers and cut the flesh into large pieces.

• Heat the remaining olive oil in a large, heavy-bottom skillet, add the eggplant flesh and bell pepper pieces and cook for 5 minutes. Add the garlic and cook for an additional 30 seconds.

• Turn all the contents of the skillet onto paper towels to drain, then transfer to the bowl of a food processor. Add the lemon rind and juice, the chopped cilantro, the paprika, and salt and pepper according to taste, and blend until a speckled purée is formed.

• Turn the eggplant and bell pepper dip into a serving bowl. Serve warm, at room temperature, or let cool for 30 minutes, then let chill in the refrigerator for at least 1 hour and serve cold. Garnish with cilantro sprigs and accompany with thick slices of bread or toast for dipping.

SERVES 8 AS PART
OF A TAPAS MEAL
1 lb 2 oz/500 g raw jumbo shrimp,
    in their shells
1 small fresh red chili

6 tbsp Spanish olive oil
2 garlic cloves, finely chopped
pinch of paprika
salt
crusty bread, to serve

Sizzling Chili Shrimp

The point of this dish is that the skillet is brought to the table and the shrimp are served really hot, hence their name. The oil should still be sizzling, and so it is usually brought to the table with a plate of bread perched on top.

• To prepare the shrimp, pull off their heads. With your fingers, peel off their shells, leaving the tails intact. Using a sharp knife, make a shallow slit along the underside of each shrimp, then pull out the dark vein and discard. Rinse the shrimp under cold water and dry well on paper towels.

• Cut the chili in half lengthwise, remove the seeds, and finely chop the flesh. It is important either to wear gloves or to wash your hands very thoroughly after chopping chilies because their juices can cause irritation to sensitive skin, especially round the eyes, nose, or mouth. Whatever you do, don't rub your eyes after touching the cut flesh of the chili.

• Heat the olive oil in a large, heavy-bottom skillet or ovenproof casserole until quite hot, then add the garlic and cook for 30 seconds. Add the shrimp, chili, paprika, and a pinch of salt and cook for 2–3 minutes, stirring all the time, until the shrimp turn pink and start to curl.

• Serve the shrimp in the cooking dish, still sizzling. Accompany with toothpicks, to spear the shrimp, and chunks or slices of crusty bread to mop up the aromatic cooking oil.

SERVES 6–8 AS PART
OF A TAPAS MEAL
7 oz/200 g manchego cheese
3 tbsp all-purpose flour
salt and pepper

1 egg
1 tsp water
1½ cups fresh white or brown
    bread crumbs
corn oil, for deep-frying

Deep-Fried Manchego Cheese

Manchego cheese is Spain's most famous cheese. It is sold at various stages of its maturity, although the most widely available is the firm, full-flavored hard cheese, as opposed to the soft, mild young cheese, which is rarely found outside Spain. Other cheeses work equally well here, such as Cheddar, mozzarella, or even a firm goat cheese.

• Slice the cheese into triangular shapes about ¾ inch/2 cm thick or alternatively into cubes measuring about the same size. Put the flour in a plastic bag and season with salt and pepper to taste. Break the egg into a shallow dish and beat together with the water. Spread the bread crumbs onto a plate.

• Toss the cheese pieces in the flour so that they are evenly coated, then dip the cheese in the egg mixture. Finally, dip the cheese in the bread crumbs so that the pieces are coated on all sides. Transfer to a large plate and store in the refrigerator until you are ready to serve them.

• Just before serving, heat about 1 inch/2.5 cm of the corn oil in a large, heavy-bottom skillet or heat the oil in a deep-fryer to 350–375°F/180–190°C, or until a cube of bread browns in 30 seconds. Add the cheese pieces, in batches of about 4 or 5 pieces so that the temperature of the oil does not drop, and deep-fry for 1–2 minutes, turning once, until the cheese is just starting to melt and they are golden brown on all sides. Do make sure that the oil is hot enough, otherwise the coating on the cheese will take too long to become crisp and the cheese inside may ooze out.

• Using a slotted spoon, remove the deep-fried cheese from the skillet or deep-fryer and drain well on paper towels. Serve the deep-fried cheese pieces hot, accompanied by toothpicks on which to spear them.

SERVES 6 AS PART
OF A TAPAS MEAL
7 oz/200 g chorizo sausage
scant 1 cup Spanish red wine

2 tbsp brandy (optional)
chopped fresh flatleaf parsley,
   to garnish
crusty bread, to serve

Chorizo in Red Wine

It is also fun to make this dish with small, individual chorizo sausages. Prepare them in exactly the same way but, after removing their outer casing, keep them whole rather than slicing. You can also use cider in place of the red wine, since it is often used in the north of Spain.

• Before you start, bear in mind that this dish is best if prepared the day before you are planning to serve it. Using a fork, prick the chorizo sausage in 3 or 4 places. Put it in a large pan and pour in the wine. Bring the wine to a boil, then lower the heat, cover, and let simmer gently for 15–20 minutes. Transfer the chorizo and wine to a bowl or dish, cover, and let the sausage marinate in the wine for 8 hours or overnight.

• The next day, remove the chorizo from the bowl or dish and reserve the wine for later. Remove the outer casing from the chorizo and cut the sausage into ¼-inch/5-mm slices. Place the slices in a large, heavy-bottom skillet or ovenproof serving dish.

• If you are adding the brandy, pour it into a small pan and heat gently. Pour the brandy over the chorizo slices, stand well back, and set alight. When the flames have died down, shake the pan gently, add the reserved wine to the pan, and cook over high heat until almost all of the wine has evaporated.

• Serve the chorizo piping hot, in the dish in which it was cooked, sprinkled with parsley to garnish. Accompany with chunks or slices of bread to mop up the juices and provide toothpicks with which to spear the chorizo.

Fresh fish and shellfish are the pride of Spanish tapas. They are eaten in vast quantities and you only have to pay a visit to a Spanish fish market to see the array of different varieties. Shrimp are popular all over Spain and you will find a dish or two on almost all tapas menus. In the north you will often find mussels, while in the south pan-fried fish is a favorite tapa. Recipes such as Lime-drizzled Shrimp, Mussels with Herb and Garlic Butter, and Calamares can be found in this chapter.

The popularity of shrimp is very much in evidence in the older-style Spanish tapas bars. One reason for this is that cutlery is not generally involved in eating tapas, so shrimp are shelled with enthusiasm and the shells discarded on the floor along with lemon seeds, toothpicks, and paper napkins. A covering of sawdust on the floor is often provided for this very reason!

FRESH FROM THE SEA

The selection of recipes in this chapter can be used for various occasions. As many tapas dishes are in fact similar to appetizers, they all make smart, elegant first courses. Simply halve the number of servings that the recipe indicates.

Just one word on cooking the fish—try not to overcook it or it will become tasteless and dry rather than remaining tender.

SERVES 6 AS PART
OF A TAPAS MEAL

2 fresh tuna steaks, weighing
about 9 oz/250 g in total and
about 1 inch/2.5 cm thick

5 tbsp Spanish olive oil

3 tbsp red wine vinegar

4 sprigs of fresh thyme,
plus extra to garnish

1 bay leaf

salt and pepper

2 tbsp all-purpose flour

1 onion, finely chopped

2 garlic cloves, finely chopped

½ cup pimiento-stuffed
green olives, sliced

crusty bread, to serve

Tuna with Pimiento-Stuffed Olives

Now that tuna can easily be bought fresh, it is a real treat. It has a firm flesh and a superb flavor. Once cooked—broiled, pan-fried, baked, or braised—you can eat it as a steak or exactly the same way as you would canned tuna.

• Don't get caught out with this recipe—the tuna steaks need to be marinated, so remember to start preparing the dish the day before you are going to serve it. Remove the skin from the tuna steaks, then cut the steaks in half along the grain of the fish. Cut each half into ½-inch/1-cm thick slices against the grain.

• Put 3 tablespoons of the olive oil and the vinegar in a large, shallow, nonmetallic dish. Strip the leaves from the sprigs of thyme and add these to the dish with the bay leaf and salt and pepper to taste. Add the prepared strips of tuna, cover the dish, and let marinate in the refrigerator for 8 hours or overnight.

• The next day, put the flour in a plastic bag. Remove the tuna strips from the marinade, reserving the marinade for later, add them to the bag of flour and toss well until they are lightly coated.

• Heat the remaining olive oil in a large, heavy-bottom skillet. Add the onion and garlic and gently cook for 5–10 minutes, or until softened and golden brown. Add the tuna strips to the skillet and cook for 2–5 minutes, turning several times, until the fish becomes opaque. Add the reserved marinade and olives to the skillet and cook for an additional 1–2 minutes, stirring, until the fish is tender and the sauce has thickened.

• Serve the tuna and olives piping hot, garnished with thyme sprigs. Accompany with chunks or slices of crusty bread for mopping up the sauce.

MAKES 12

12 oz/350 g white fish fillets, such as
    cod, haddock, or angler fish

1¼ cups milk

salt and pepper

4 tbsp olive oil or 2 oz/55 g butter

scant ½ cup all-purpose flour

4 tbsp capers, coarsely chopped

1 tsp paprika

1 garlic clove, crushed

1 tsp lemon juice

3 tbsp chopped fresh flatleaf parsley,
    plus extra sprigs to garnish

1 egg, beaten

1 cup fresh white bread crumbs

1 tbsp sesame seeds

corn oil, for deep-frying

lemon wedges, to garnish

mayonnaise, to serve

Cod and Caper Croquettes

The secret of cooking croquettes successfully is to chill the mixture in the refrigerator before cooking. You will then find that they don't disintegrate when put in the hot oil. As a matter of interest, Spain is the world's largest producer of capers!

• Put the fish fillets in a large, heavy-bottom skillet. Pour in the milk and season to taste with salt and pepper. Bring to a boil, then lower the heat, cover the skillet, and let simmer gently for 8–10 minutes, or until the fish flakes easily when tested with a fork. Using a spatula, remove the fish fillets from the skillet. Pour the milk into a pitcher and set aside for later. Flake the fish, removing and discarding the skin and bones.

• Heat the olive oil or butter in a pan. Stir in the flour to form a paste and cook gently, stirring, for 1 minute. Remove the pan from the heat and gradually stir in the reserved milk until smooth. Return to the heat and slowly bring to a boil, stirring all the time, until the mixture thickens.

• Remove the pan from the heat, add the flaked fish, and beat until the mixture is smooth. Add the capers, paprika, garlic, lemon juice, and parsley and mix well together. Season the mixture to taste with salt and pepper. Spread the fish mixture in a dish and let stand until cool, then cover and put in the refrigerator for 2–3 hours or overnight.

• When the fish mixture has chilled, pour the beaten egg onto a plate. Put the bread crumbs and sesame seeds on a separate plate, mix together, and spread out. Divide the fish mixture into 12 equal-size portions. Then, with lightly floured hands, form each portion into a sausage shape, measuring about 3 inches/7.5 cm in length. Dip the croquettes, one at a time, in the beaten egg, roll in the bread crumb mixture to coat them. Place on a plate and let chill for about 1 hour.

• To cook the croquettes, heat the oil in a deep-fryer to 350–375°F/180–190°C, or until a cube of bread browns in 30 seconds. Add the croquettes, in batches, and deep-fry for 3 minutes, or until golden brown and crispy. Remove from the pan with a slotted spoon and drain well on paper towels.

• Serve piping hot, garnished with lemon wedges and parsley sprigs, and accompanied by a bowl of mayonnaise for dipping.

MAKES 12
12 oz/350 g angler fish tail or
    9 oz/250 g angler fish fillet
12 stalks of fresh rosemary
3 tbsp Spanish olive oil
juice of ½ small lemon

1 garlic clove, crushed
salt and pepper
6 thick slices Canadian bacon
lemon wedges, to garnish
Aïoli (see page 92), to serve

Angler Fish, Rosemary, and Bacon Skewers

Angler fish is ideal for skewers because of its firm texture, but other firm-fleshed fish, such as cod, swordfish, or tuna, would make ideal alternatives. Instead of using rosemary stalks, you can use the more traditional metal skewers or wooden bamboo skewers. The latter should be presoaked in cold water for 30 minutes to prevent them burning.

• If using angler fish tail, cut either side of the central bone with a sharp knife and remove the flesh to form 2 fillets. Slice the fillets in half lengthwise, then cut each fillet into 12 bite-size chunks to give a total of 24 pieces. Put the angler fish pieces in a large bowl.

• To prepare the skewers, strip the leaves off the rosemary stalks and set them aside, just leaving a few leaves at one end.

• For the marinade, finely chop the reserved leaves and whisk together in a bowl with the olive oil, lemon juice, garlic, and salt and pepper to taste. Add the angler fish pieces and toss until coated in the marinade. Cover and let marinate in the refrigerator for 1–2 hours.

• Cut each bacon slice in half lengthwise, then in half widthwise, and roll up each piece. Thread 2 pieces of angler fish alternately with 2 bacon rolls onto the prepared rosemary skewers.

• Preheat the broiler, grill pan, or barbecue. If you are cooking the skewers under a broiler, arrange them on the broiler pan so that the leaves of the rosemary skewers protrude from the broiler and therefore do not catch fire during cooking. Broil the angler fish and bacon skewers for 10 minutes, turning from time to time and basting with any remaining marinade, or until cooked. Serve hot, garnished with lemon wedges for squeezing over them and accompanied by a bowl of Aïoli in which to dip them.

SERVES 6 AS PART
OF A TAPAS MEAL
1 lb/450 g prepared squid (see Note)
all-purpose flour, for coating

corn oil, for deep-frying
salt
lemon wedges, to garnish
Aïoli (see page 92), to serve

Calamares

Squid is available already prepared and sliced into rings. If you need to prepare the squid yourself, hold the body in one hand and pull on the head and tentacles with the other. The body contents will come away too and can be discarded. Cut off the edible tentacles just above the eyes and discard the head. Carefully remove the ink sacs from the head. Finally, remove the backbone and peel off the thin, dark outer skin.

• Slice the squid into ½-inch/1-cm rings and halve the tentacles if large. Rinse and dry well on paper towels so that they do not spit during cooking. Dust the squid rings with flour so that they are lightly coated. Do not season the flour, as Spanish cooks will tell you that seasoning squid with salt before cooking toughens it. They should know!

• Heat the corn oil in a deep-fryer to 350–375°F/180–190°C, or until a cube of bread browns in 30 seconds. Carefully add the squid rings, in batches so that the temperature of the oil does not drop, and deep-fry for 2–3 minutes, or until golden brown and crisp all over, turning several times. Do not overcook as the squid will become tough and rubbery rather than moist and tender.

• Using a slotted spoon, remove the deep-fried squid from the deep-fryer and drain well on paper towels. Transfer to a warm oven while you deep-fry the remaining squid rings.

• Sprinkle the deep-fried squid with salt and serve piping hot, garnished with lemon wedges for squeezing over them. Accompany with a bowl of Aïoli in which to dip the pieces.

SERVES 6 AS PART
OF A TAPAS MEAL

12 small fresh sardines

¾ cup Spanish olive oil

4 tbsp sherry vinegar

2 carrots, cut into julienne strips

1 onion, thinly sliced

1 garlic clove, crushed

1 bay leaf

salt and pepper

4 tbsp chopped fresh flatleaf parsley

few sprigs of fresh dill, to garnish

lemon wedges, to serve

Sardines Marinated in Sherry Vinegar

Fresh trout or salmon fillets can be given the same treatment, but instead of pan-frying the fish, it is better to steam the fillets for 5 minutes, or until tender. When cooked, slice each fillet in half lengthwise. You will need 6 fish fillets for this recipe.

• If it has not already been done, clean the fish by scraping the scales off with a knife, being careful not to cut the skin. The choice is yours whether you then leave the heads and tails on or cut them off and discard. Slit along the belly of each fish and remove the innards under cold running water. Then, dry each fish well on paper towels.

• Heat 4 tablespoons of the olive oil in a large, heavy-bottom skillet. Add the sardines and cook for 10 minutes, or until browned on both sides. Using a spatula, very carefully remove the sardines from the skillet and transfer to a large, shallow, nonmetallic dish that will hold the sardines in a single layer.

• Gently heat the remaining olive oil and the sherry vinegar in a large pan, add the carrot strips, onion, garlic, and bay leaf and let simmer gently for 5 minutes, until softened. Season the vegetables to taste with salt and pepper. Let the mixture cool slightly, then pour the marinade over the sardines.

• Cover the dish and let the sardines cool before transferring to the refrigerator. Let marinate for about 8 hours or overnight, spooning the marinade over the sardines occasionally, although there is no necessity to get up in the middle of the night! Return the sardines to room temperature before serving, sprinkle with parsley, and garnish with dill sprigs. Serve with lemon wedges.

SERVES 8 AS PART
OF A TAPAS MEAL
4 fresh salmon fillets, weighing
    about 1 lb 10 oz/750 g in total
salt and pepper
3 tbsp Spanish olive oil
1 fresh flatleaf parsley sprig,
    to garnish

MOJO SAUCE
2 garlic cloves, peeled
2 tsp paprika
1 tsp ground cumin
5 tbsp Spanish extra virgin olive oil
2 tbsp white wine vinegar
salt

Fresh Salmon in Mojo Sauce

Mojo Sauce is also known as Canary Island Red Sauce, after its place of origin. When served without the paprika but with finely chopped fresh cilantro and parsley leaves, it is known as Canary Island Green Sauce. It is also good drizzled over boiled new potatoes.

• To prepare the Mojo Sauce, put the garlic, paprika, and cumin in the bowl of a food processor fitted with the metal blade and, using a pulsing action, blend for 1 minute to mix well together. With the motor still running, add 1 tablespoon of the olive oil, drop by drop, through the feeder tube. When it has been added, scrape down the sides of the bowl with a spatula, then very slowly continue to pour in the oil in a thin, steady stream, until all the oil has been added and the sauce has slightly thickened. Add the vinegar and blend for an additional 1 minute. Season the sauce with salt to taste.

• To prepare the salmon, remove the skin, cut each fillet in half widthwise, then cut lengthwise into ¾-inch/2-cm thick slices, discarding any bones. Season the pieces of fish to taste with salt and pepper.

• Heat the olive oil in a large, heavy-bottom skillet. When hot, add the pieces of fish and cook for about 10 minutes, depending on its thickness, turning occasionally until cooked and browned on both sides.

• Transfer the salmon to a warmed serving dish, drizzle over some of the Mojo Sauce, and serve hot, garnished with parsley, and accompanied by the remaining sauce in a small serving bowl.

SERVES 8 AS PART
OF A TAPAS MEAL
⅔ cup dry white wine
⅔ cup fish stock
large pinch of saffron threads
2 lb/900 g shelled scallops,
   preferably large ones
salt and pepper

3 tbsp Spanish olive oil
1 small onion, finely chopped
2 garlic cloves, finely chopped
⅔ cup heavy cream
squeeze of lemon juice
chopped fresh flatleaf parsley,
   to garnish
crusty bread, to serve

Scallops in Saffron Sauce

Shelled scallops are available, both fresh and frozen, from supermarkets and fish stores. Should you buy them from a fish store, ask if you can have some shells, as they make attractive serving dishes. You will need to scrub them clean before use.

• Put the wine, fish stock, and saffron in a pan and bring to a boil. Lower the heat, cover, and let simmer gently for 15 minutes.
• Meanwhile, remove and discard from each scallop the tough, white muscle that is found opposite the coral, and separate the coral from the scallop. Slice the scallops vertically into thick slices, including the corals if they are present. Dry the scallops well on paper towels, then season to taste with salt and pepper.
• Heat the olive oil in a large, heavy-bottom skillet. Add the onion and garlic and cook for 5 minutes, or until softened and lightly browned. Add the sliced scallops to the skillet and cook gently for 5 minutes, stirring occasionally, or until they turn just opaque. The secret is not to overcook the scallops, otherwise they will become tough and rubbery.
• Using a slotted spoon, remove the scallops from the skillet and transfer to a warmed plate. Add the saffron liquid to the skillet, bring to a boil, and boil rapidly until reduced to about half. Lower the heat and gradually stir in the cream, just a little at a time. Let simmer gently until the sauce thickens.
• Return the scallops to the skillet and let simmer for 1–2 minutes just to heat them through. Add a squeeze of lemon juice and season to taste with salt and pepper. Serve the scallops hot, garnished with the parsley, and accompanied by chunks or slices of crusty bread to mop up the saffron sauce.

SERVES 6 AS PART
OF A TAPAS MEAL
4 limes
12 raw jumbo shrimp, in their shells
3 tbsp Spanish olive oil

2 garlic cloves, finely chopped
splash of fino sherry
salt and pepper
4 tbsp chopped fresh flatleaf parsley

Lime-Drizzled Shrimp

This dish can also be prepared with cooked fresh or frozen shrimp. Make sure that you dry them very well on paper towels before using and, as they are already cooked, add them to the skillet for just 1–2 minutes, to heat them through.

• Grate the rind and squeeze the juice from 2 of the limes. Cut the remaining 2 limes into wedges and set them aside for later.

• To prepare the shrimp, remove the head and legs, leaving the shells and tails intact. Using a sharp knife, make a shallow slit along the underside of each shrimp, then pull out the dark vein and discard. Rinse the shrimp under cold water and dry well on paper towels.

• Heat the olive oil in a large, heavy-bottom skillet, then add the garlic and cook for 30 seconds. Add the shrimp and cook for 5 minutes, stirring from time to time, or until they turn pink and start to curl. Mix in the lime rind, juice, and a splash of sherry to moisten, then stir well together.

• Transfer the cooked shrimp to a serving dish, season to taste with salt and pepper, and sprinkle with the parsley. Serve piping hot, accompanied by the reserved lime wedges for squeezing over the shrimp.

SERVES 8 AS PART
OF A TAPAS MEAL
1 lb 12 oz/800 g fresh mussels,
   in their shells
splash of dry white wine
1 bay leaf
3 oz/85 g butter
generous ½ cup fresh white
   or brown bread crumbs

4 tbsp chopped fresh flatleaf parsley,
   plus extra sprigs to garnish
2 tbsp snipped fresh chives
2 garlic cloves, finely chopped
salt and pepper
lemon wedges, to serve

Mussels with Herb and Garlic Butter

Due to the lack of lush pastureland in most of Spain, dairy cattle are not extensively raised and therefore oil, as opposed to butter, is more commonly used in cooking. Nevertheless, butter is occasionally used, as in this recipe.

• Clean the mussels by scrubbing or scraping the shells and pulling out any beards that are attached to them. Discard any with broken shells and any that refuse to close when tapped. Put the mussels in a strainer and rinse well under cold running water. Preheat the oven to 450°F/230°C.
• Put the mussels in a large pan and add a splash of wine and the bay leaf. Cook, covered, over high heat for 5 minutes, shaking the pan occasionally, or until the mussels are opened. Drain the mussels and discard any that remain closed.
• Shell the mussels, reserving one half of each shell. Arrange the mussels, in their half shells, in a large, shallow, ovenproof serving dish.
• Melt the butter and pour into a small bowl. Add the bread crumbs, parsley, chives, garlic, and salt and pepper to taste and mix well together. Let stand until the butter has set slightly. Using your fingers or 2 teaspoons, take a large pinch of the herb and butter mixture and use to fill each mussel shell, pressing it down well. You can chill the filled mussels in the refrigerator at this point until ready to serve.
• To serve, bake the mussels in the oven for 10 minutes, or until hot. Serve immediately, garnished with parsley sprigs, and accompanied by lemon wedges for squeezing over them.

MAKES 24
1 tbsp Spanish olive oil
1 small onion, finely chopped
1 garlic clove, finely chopped
splash of dry white wine
2 eggs
2/3 cup milk or light cream
6 oz/175 g canned crabmeat, drained

1/2 cup manchego or Parmesan
    cheese, grated
2 tbsp chopped fresh flatleaf parsley
pinch of freshly grated nutmeg
salt and pepper
sprigs of fresh dill, to garnish

PIE DOUGH
2¼ cups all-purpose flour,
    plus extra for dusting
pinch of salt
6 oz/175 g butter
2 tbsp cold water

OR
1 lb 2 oz/500 g ready-made
    unsweetened pastry

Crab Tartlets

You only have to look along the shelves of a Spanish supermarket to see the numerous varieties of canned fish that are available. On that note, canned salmon or tuna could easily be used in this recipe in place of the crabmeat.

• Preheat the oven to 375°F/190°C. To prepare the crabmeat filling, heat the olive oil in a heavy-bottom skillet, add the onion and cook for 5 minutes, or until softened but not browned. Add the garlic and cook for an additional 30 seconds. Add a splash of wine and cook for 1–2 minutes, or until most of the wine has evaporated.
• Lightly whisk the eggs in a large mixing bowl, then whisk in the milk or cream. Add the crabmeat, cheese, and parsley, and the onion mixture. Season the mixture with nutmeg and salt and pepper to taste and mix well.
• To prepare the pie dough if you are making it yourself, mix the flour and salt together in a large mixing bowl. Add the butter, cut into small pieces, and rub in until the mixture resembles fine bread crumbs. Gradually stir in enough of the water to form a firm dough. Alternatively, the pie dough could be made in a food processor.
• On a lightly floured counter, thinly roll out the dough. Using a plain, round 2¾-inch/7-cm cutter, cut the pastry into 18 circles. Gently pile the trimmings together, roll out again, then cut out an additional 6 circles. Use to line 24 x 1½-inch/4-cm tartlet pans. Carefully spoon the crabmeat mixture into the pastry shells, taking care not to overfill them.
• Bake the tartlets in the oven for 25–30 minutes, or until golden brown and set. Serve the crab tartlets hot or cold, garnished with fresh dill sprigs.

This chapter includes some of Spain's most popular tapas dishes. Eggs are an instant tapa on their own and a selection of tapas dishes, particularly in the south of Spain, would be incomplete without Deviled Eggs. A wedge of the thick potato omelet, Tortilla Española, has to be Spain's most popular egg dish.

Cubes of cheese are another instant tapa. Spain produces many cheeses, but the one that is the most easy to obtain outside Spain is manchego, which is made from sheep's milk. If you are unable to find it, then use freshly cut Italian Parmesan cheese.

Meat dishes are included here too and, although meat has never been plentiful in Spain, pork is a popular meat, as are cured serrano ham and chicken. The Chicken Livers in Sherry Sauce is a firm favorite! Chorizo, flavored with paprika and garlic, is

EGG, CHEESE, AND MEAT MORSELS

Spain's favorite sausage, and can be eaten cold or pan-fried, baked, or cooked in a sauce. If possible, serve these meat tapas dishes in small, earthenware bowls, just as they are seen on every bar counter in Spain. These dishes retain the heat or cold well, so will keep your tapas dish at the correct temperature. If you don't have any, don't worry! Ordinary serving dishes will serve the purpose equally well. These meat tapas also make delicious light lunch or supper dishes. Simply halve the number that the recipe suggests it will serve and accompany with some good fresh country bread to mop up the juices.

SERVES 8 AS PART
OF A TAPAS MEAL
1 lb/450 g waxy potatoes
scant 2 cups Spanish olive oil
2 onions, chopped

2 large eggs
salt and pepper
sprigs of fresh flatleaf parsley,
    to garnish

Tortilla Española

This is Spain's classic tapas dish (as well as the staple food for a picnic) and is made with potato, onion, and egg. Other ingredients can be added, such as ham, bacon, cheese, mushrooms, red or green bell peppers, and asparagus, but the Spanish prefer to keep it plain.

• Peel the potatoes, cut into small cubes or wedges, then put on a clean dish towel and dry well. Heat the olive oil in a large, heavy-bottom or nonstick skillet. Add the potato pieces and onions, then lower the heat and cook the potatoes, stirring frequently so that they do not clump together, for 20 minutes, or until they are tender but not browned. The secret of success is to cook the potatoes for a long time so that they absorb the flavor of the oil and are cooked but not browned or crisp, and do not fall apart. They are in fact almost boiled rather than pan-fried.

• Meanwhile, beat the eggs lightly in a large bowl and season well with salt and pepper. Place a strainer over a large bowl.

• When the potatoes and onions are cooked, drain them into the strainer so that the bowl catches the oil. Set the oil aside. When the potatoes and onions are well drained, gently stir them into the beaten eggs.

• Wipe the skillet clean or wash it if necessary to prevent the tortilla sticking. Heat 2 tablespoons of the reserved olive oil in the skillet. When hot, add the egg and potato mixture, lower the heat and cook for 3–5 minutes, or until the underside is just set. Use a spatula to push the potatoes down into the egg so that they are completely submerged and keep loosening the tortilla from the bottom of the skillet to stop it sticking.

• To cook the second side of the tortilla, cover it with a plate, and hold the plate in place with the other hand. Drain off the oil in the skillet, then quickly turn the skillet upside down so that the tortilla falls on to the plate. Return the skillet to the heat and add a little more of the reserved oil to it if necessary. Slide the tortilla, cooked side uppermost, back into the skillet and cook for an additional 3–5 minutes, or until set underneath. The tortilla is cooked when it is firm and crisp on the outside but still slightly runny in the center.

• Slide the tortilla onto a serving plate and let stand for about 15 minutes. Serve it warm or cold, cut into small squares, fingers, or wedges, and garnished with parsley sprigs.

MAKES 16

8 large eggs

2 whole pimientos (sweet red peppers) from a jar or can

8 green olives

5 tbsp mayonnaise

8 drops Tabasco sauce

large pinch cayenne pepper

salt and pepper

paprika, for dusting

sprigs of fresh dill, to garnish

Deviled Eggs

In the south of Spain, the selection of dishes served in tapas bars would be considered incomplete without the inclusion of these Deviled Eggs and Tortilla Española (see page 54). As a variation, you could use rolled, canned anchovies to garnish each egg.

• To cook the eggs, put them in a pan, cover with cold water, and slowly bring to a boil. Immediately reduce the heat to very low, cover, and let simmer gently for 10 minutes. As soon as the eggs are cooked, drain, and put under cold running water. By doing this quickly, it will prevent a black ring from forming round the egg yolk. Gently tap the eggs to crack the eggshells and let them stand until cold. When cold, crack the shells all over and remove them.

• Using a stainless steel knife, halve the eggs lengthwise, then carefully remove the yolks. Put the yolks in a nylon strainer, set over a bowl, and rub through, then mash them with a wooden spoon or fork. If necessary, rinse the egg whites under cold water and dry very carefully.

• Put the pimientos on paper towels to dry well, then chop them finely, reserving a few strips. Finely chop the olives. If you are going to pipe the filling into the eggs, you need to chop both these ingredients very finely so that they will go through a 1/2-inch/1-cm tip. Add the chopped pimientos and most of the chopped olives to the mashed egg yolks, reserving 16 larger pieces to garnish. Add the mayonnaise, mix well together, then add the Tabasco sauce, cayenne pepper, and salt and pepper to taste.

• For a grand finale, put the egg yolk mixture into a pastry bag fitted with a 1/2-inch/1-cm plain tip and pipe the mixture into the hollow egg whites. Alternatively, for a simpler finish, use a teaspoon to spoon the prepared filling into each egg half.

• Arrange the eggs on a serving plate. Add a small strip of the reserved pimientos and a piece of olive to the top of each stuffed egg. Dust with a little paprika and garnish with dill sprigs.

MAKES 26

3 oz/85 g firm or soft cheese
(see Note)

½ cup pitted green olives

¼ cup sundried tomatoes in oil,
drained

1¾ oz/50 g canned anchovies,
drained

pepper

2 tbsp sundried tomato paste

all-purpose flour, for dusting

1 lb 2 oz/500 g ready-made puff
pastry, thawed if frozen

beaten egg, to glaze

Cheese and Olive Empanadillas

Since there are not many Spanish cheeses available outside Spain, you can choose to make these pastries with manchego, Cheddar, Gruyère, Gouda, mozzarella, or a firm goat cheese. Large versions of these empanadillas are known as empanadas.

• Preheat the oven to 400°F/200°C. Cut the cheese into small dice measuring about ¼ inch/5 mm. Chop the olives, sundried tomatoes, and anchovies into pieces about the same size as the cheese. Put all the chopped ingredients in a bowl, season with pepper to taste, and gently mix together. Stir in the sundried tomato paste.

• On a lightly floured counter, thinly roll out the puff pastry. Using a plain, round 3¼-inch/8-cm cutter, cut into 18 circles. Gently pile the trimmings together, roll out again, then cut out an additional 8 circles. Using a teaspoon, put a little of the prepared filling equally in the center of each of the pastry circles.

• Dampen the edges of the pastry with a little water, then bring up the sides to completely cover the filling and pinch the edges together with your fingers to seal them. With the tip of a sharp knife, make a small slit in the top of each pastry. You can store the pastries in the refrigerator at this stage until you are ready to bake them.

• Place the pastries onto dampened baking sheets and brush each with a little beaten egg to glaze. Bake in the oven for 10–15 minutes, or until golden brown, crisp and well risen. Serve the empanadillas piping hot, warm, or cold.

SERVES 8 AS PART
OF A TAPAS MEAL
scant ½ cup all-purpose flour
¼ cup Spanish olive oil
⅔ cup water
2 eggs, beaten
½ cup manchego, Parmesan,
    Cheddar, Gouda, or Gruyère
    cheese, finely grated

½ tsp paprika
salt and pepper
corn oil, for deep-frying

FIERY TOMATO SALSA
2 tbsp Spanish olive oil
1 small onion, finely chopped
1 garlic clove, crushed
splash of dry white wine

14 oz/400 g canned chopped
    tomatoes
1 tbsp tomato paste
¼–½ tsp dried red pepper flakes
dash of Tabasco sauce
pinch of sugar
salt and pepper

Cheese Puffs with Fiery Tomato Salsa

These crisp little cheese puffs are light and fluffy, and although in this recipe they are served with a salsa, they can, if preferred, simply be accompanied by small tea melons. Serve these speared on toothpicks so that a tea melon and a cheese puff can be eaten together.

• To make the salsa, heat the olive oil in a pan, add the onion and cook for 5 minutes, or until softened but not browned. Add the garlic and cook for an additional 30 seconds. Add the wine and let bubble, then add all the remaining salsa ingredients to the pan and let simmer, uncovered, for 10–15 minutes, or until a thick sauce is formed. Spoon into a serving bowl and set aside until ready to serve.

• Meanwhile, prepare the cheese puffs. Sift the flour onto a plate or sheet of waxed paper. Put the olive oil and water in a pan and slowly bring to a boil. As soon as the water boils, remove the pan from the heat, and quickly tip in the flour all at once. Using a wooden spoon, beat the mixture until it is smooth and leaves the sides of the pan.

• Let the mixture cool for 1–2 minutes, then gradually add the eggs, beating hard after each addition and keeping the mixture stiff. Add the cheese and paprika, season to taste with salt and pepper, and mix well together. You can store the mixture in the refrigerator at this stage until you are ready to deep-fry the cheese puffs.

• Just before serving the cheese puffs, heat the corn oil in a deep-fryer to 350–375°F/ 180–190°C, or until a cube of bread browns in 30 seconds. Drop teaspoonfuls of the prepared mixture, in batches, into the hot oil and deep-fry for 2–3 minutes, turning once, or until golden and crispy. They should rise to the surface of the oil and puff up. Drain well on paper towels.

• Serve the puffs piping hot, accompanied by the fiery salsa for dipping, and toothpicks to spear the puffs.

MAKES 12
4½ oz/125 g chorizo sausage,
    outer casing removed
all-purpose flour, for dusting

9 oz/250 g ready-made puff pastry,
    thawed if frozen
beaten egg, to glaze
paprika, to garnish

Chorizo Empanadillas

A tapas meal would not be complete without the inclusion of chorizo! In this recipe it is encased in puff pastry and makes a delicious accompaniment to a glass of chilled white wine. The empanadillas are particularly easy to prepare—in fact something a child might like to make. Just watch that they don't eat all the chorizo before it reaches the oven!

• Preheat the oven to 400°F/200°C. Cut the chorizo sausage into small dice measuring about ½ inch/1 cm square. On a lightly floured counter, thinly roll out the puff pastry. Using a plain, round 3¼-inch/8-cm cutter, cut into circles. Gently pile the trimmings together, roll out again, then cut out additional circles to produce 12 in total. Put about a teaspoonful of the chopped chorizo onto each of the pastry circles.

• Dampen the edges of the pastry with a little water, then fold one half over the other half to completely cover the chorizo. Seal the edges together with your fingers. Using the prongs of a fork, press against the edges to give a decorative finish and seal them further. With the tip of a sharp knife, make a small slit in the side of each pastry. You can store the pastries in the refrigerator at this stage until you are ready to bake them.

• Place the pastries onto dampened baking sheets and brush each with a little beaten egg to glaze. Bake in the oven for 10–15 minutes, or until golden brown and puffed. Using a small strainer, lightly dust the top of each empanadilla with a little paprika to garnish. Serve the chorizo empanadillas hot or warm.

SERVES 6–8 AS PART
OF A TAPAS MEAL
2 oz/55 g white or brown bread,
   crusts removed
3 tbsp water
2 cups fresh lean ground pork
   (see Note)
1 large onion, finely chopped
1 garlic clove, crushed

2 tbsp chopped fresh flatleaf parsley,
   plus extra to garnish
1 egg, beaten
freshly grated nutmeg
salt and pepper
flour, for coating
2 tbsp Spanish olive oil
squeeze of lemon juice
crusty bread, to serve

ALMOND SAUCE
2 tbsp Spanish olive oil
1 oz/25 g white or brown bread
2/3 cup blanched almonds
2 garlic cloves, finely chopped
2/3 cup dry white wine
salt and pepper
scant 2 cups vegetable stock

Tiny Spanish Meatballs in Almond Sauce

Ground pork, or a combination of pork and veal, is the most traditional meat used in Spain to make these meatballs, but there is no reason why you could not use ground lamb or beef, if preferred.

• To prepare the meatballs, put the bread in a bowl, add the water, and let soak for 5 minutes. With your hands, squeeze out the water and return the bread to the dried bowl. Add the pork, onion, garlic, parsley, and egg, then season generously with grated nutmeg and a little salt and pepper. Knead the ingredients well together to form a smooth mixture.

• Spread some flour on a plate. With floured hands, shape the meat mixture into about 30 equal-size balls, then roll each meatball in flour until coated.

• Heat the olive oil in a large, heavy-bottom skillet, add the meatballs, in batches so that they do not overcrowd the skillet, and cook for 4–5 minutes, or until browned on all sides. Using a slotted spoon, remove the meatballs from the skillet and set aside.

• To make the Almond Sauce, heat the olive oil in the same skillet in which the meatballs were cooked. Break the bread into small pieces, add to the skillet with the almonds and cook gently, stirring frequently, until the bread and almonds are golden brown. Add the garlic and cook for an additional 30 seconds, then pour in the wine and boil for 1–2 minutes. Season to taste with salt and pepper and let cool slightly.

• Transfer the almond mixture to a food processor. Pour in the vegetable stock and blend the mixture until smooth. Return the sauce to the skillet.

• Carefully add the cooked meatballs to the almond sauce and let simmer for 25 minutes, or until the meatballs are tender. Taste the sauce and season with salt and pepper if necessary.

• Transfer the cooked meatballs and almond sauce to a warmed serving dish, then add a squeeze of lemon juice to taste and sprinkle with chopped parsley to garnish. Serve piping hot, accompanied by chunks or slices of crusty bread for mopping up the Almond Sauce.

MAKES 12

1 lb/450 g lean boneless pork
   (see Note)

3 tbsp Spanish olive oil, plus extra
   for oiling (optional)

grated rind and juice of 1 large lemon

2 garlic cloves, crushed

2 tbsp chopped fresh flatleaf parsley,
   plus extra to garnish

1 tbsp ras-el-hanout spice blend
   (see Note)

salt and pepper

Miniature Pork Brochettes

Although usually made with pork in Spain, these brochettes are of Arab origin, and would be made using lamb; both are delicious. The ras-el-hanout spice blend, found in delicatessens and larger supermarkets, consists of galangal, rosebuds, black peppercorns, ginger, cardamom, nigella, cayenne, allspice, lavender, cinnamon, cassia, coriander, mace, nutmeg, and cloves!

• The brochettes are marinated overnight, so remember to do this in advance in order that they are ready when you need them. Cut the pork into pieces about ¾ inch/2 cm square and put in a large, shallow, nonmetallic dish that will hold the pieces in a single layer.

• To prepare the marinade, put all the remaining ingredients in a bowl and mix well together. Pour the marinade over the pork and toss the meat in it until well coated. Cover the dish and let marinate in the refrigerator for 8 hours or overnight, stirring the pork 2–3 times.

• You can use either wooden or metal skewers to cook the brochettes and for this recipe you will need about 12 x 6-inch/15-cm skewers. If you are using wooden ones, soak them in cold water for about 30 minutes prior to using. This helps to stop them burning and the food sticking to them during cooking. Metal skewers simply need to be greased, and flat ones should be used in preference to round ones to prevent the food on them falling off.

• Preheat the broiler, grill pan, or barbecue. Thread 3 marinated pork pieces, leaving a little space between each piece, onto each prepared skewer. Cook the brochettes for 10–15 minutes, or until tender and lightly charred, turning several times and basting with the remaining marinade during cooking. Serve the pork brochettes piping hot, garnished with parsley.

SERVES 6–8 AS PART
OF A TAPAS MEAL
4 large skinless, boneless
    chicken breasts
5 tbsp Spanish olive oil
1 onion, finely chopped
6 garlic cloves, finely chopped

grated rind of 1 lemon, finely pared
    rind of 1 lemon and juice of both
    lemons
4 tbsp chopped fresh flatleaf parsley,
    plus extra to garnish
salt and pepper
lemon wedges and crusty bread,
    to serve

Chicken in Lemon and Garlic

There are several variations to this popular, quick, and easy-to-prepare tapas dish. Try, for example, using chicken wings or, in place of the chicken, use slices of fresh rabbit, turkey, or pork.

• Using a sharp knife, slice the chicken breasts widthwise into very thin slices. Heat the olive oil in a large, heavy-bottom skillet, add the onion and cook for 5 minutes, or until softened but not browned. Add the garlic and cook for an additional 30 seconds.

• Add the sliced chicken to the skillet and cook gently for 5–10 minutes, stirring from time to time, until all the ingredients are lightly browned and the chicken is tender.

• Add the grated lemon rind and the lemon juice and let it bubble. At the same time, deglaze the skillet by scraping and stirring all the bits on the bottom of the skillet into the juices with a wooden spoon. Remove the skillet from the heat, stir in the parsley, and season to taste with salt and pepper.

• Transfer the chicken in lemon and garlic, piping hot, to a warmed serving dish. Sprinkle with the pared lemon rind, garnish with the parsley, and serve with lemon wedges for squeezing over the chicken, accompanied by chunks or slices of crusty bread for mopping up the lemon and garlic juices.

MAKES 8

4 tbsp olive oil or 2 oz/55 g butter

4 tbsp all-purpose flour

scant 1 cup milk

4 oz/115 g cooked chicken, ground

2 oz/55 g serrano or cooked ham,
   very finely chopped

1 tbsp chopped fresh flatleaf parsley,
   plus extra sprigs to garnish

small pinch of freshly grated nutmeg

salt and pepper

1 egg, beaten

1 cup day-old white bread crumbs

corn oil, for deep-frying

Aïoli (see page 92), to serve

Crispy Chicken and Ham Croquettes

These crispy croquettes are another very popular tapas served all over Spain and come in an enormous variety of flavors, including Cod and Caper Croquettes (see page 34), and in all shapes and sizes.

• Heat the olive oil or butter in a pan. Stir in the flour to form a paste and cook gently for 1 minute, stirring constantly. Remove the pan from the heat and gradually stir in the milk until smooth. Return to the heat and slowly bring to a boil, stirring all the time, until the mixture boils and thickens.

• Remove the pan from the heat, add the ground chicken, and beat until the mixture is smooth. Add the chopped ham, parsley, and nutmeg and mix well together. Season the mixture to taste with salt and pepper. Spread the chicken mixture in a dish and let stand for 30 minutes, until cool, then cover and put in the refrigerator for 2–3 hours or overnight. Don't be tempted to miss out this stage, as chilling the croquettes helps to stop them falling apart when they are cooked.

• When the chicken mixture has chilled, pour the beaten egg onto a plate and spread out the bread crumbs on a separate plate. Divide the chicken mixture into 8 equal-size portions. With dampened hands, form each portion into a cylindrical shape. Dip the croquettes, one at a time, in the beaten egg, then roll in the bread crumbs to coat them. Place on a plate and let chill in the refrigerator for about 1 hour.

• To cook the croquettes, heat the oil in a deep-fryer to 350–375°F/180–190°C, or until a cube of bread browns in 30 seconds. Add the croquettes, in batches to prevent the temperature of the oil dropping, and deep-fry for 5–10 minutes, or until golden brown and crispy. Remove from the pan with a slotted spoon and drain well on paper towels.

• Serve the croquettes piping hot, garnished with parsley sprigs, and accompanied by a bowl of Aïoli for dipping.

SERVES 6 AS PART
OF A TAPAS MEAL
1 lb/450 g chicken livers
2 tbsp Spanish olive oil
1 small onion, finely chopped

2 garlic cloves, finely chopped
generous ⅓ cup dry Spanish sherry
salt and pepper
2 tbsp chopped fresh flatleaf parsley
crusty bread or toast, to serve

Chicken Livers in Sherry Sauce

This tapas dish is often served in Andalucia's tapas bars and is equally popular made with lamb's or calf's kidneys. For a variation, you could add some quartered mushrooms and/or 1 tablespoon of drained capers or chopped green olives.

• If necessary, trim the chicken livers, cutting away any ducts and gristle, then cut them into small, bite-size pieces. Heat the olive oil in a large, heavy-bottom skillet. Add the onion and cook for 5 minutes, or until softened but not browned. Add the garlic and cook for an additional 30 seconds.

• Add the chicken livers to the skillet and cook for 2–3 minutes, stirring all the time, until they are firm and have changed color on the outside but are still pink and soft in the center. Using a slotted spoon, lift the chicken livers from the pan, transfer them to a large, warmed serving dish or several smaller ones, and keep warm.

• Add the sherry to the skillet, increase the heat, and let it bubble for 3–4 minutes to evaporate the alcohol and reduce slightly. At the same time, deglaze the skillet by scraping and stirring all the bits on the bottom of the skillet into the sauce with a wooden spoon. Season the sauce to taste with salt and pepper.

• Pour the sherry sauce over the chicken livers and sprinkle over the parsley. Serve piping hot, accompanied by chunks or slices of crusty bread or toast to mop up the sherry sauce.

There are many tapas dishes that are based on vegetables, which in Spain are treated with loving care. The Spanish serve tapas vegetable dishes when the vegetables are in season and you should do the same. The Roasted Asparagus with Mountain Ham dish should, for example, appear on your table in spring!

The recipe for Stuffed Pimientos is very flexible—it includes a choice of two different fillings, but you can experiment with other fillings of your own depending on the tastes of your guests. Another vegetable dish that should not be overlooked is the Russian Salad served in tapas bars all over Spain. Do not think of the once-popular canned vegetable concoction of the same name, since it is only the name that has any resemblance. It can, incidentally, also be served as a meal in its own right.

THE VEGETABLE CONNECTION

Potato dishes are particularly popular tapas and there are several here to choose from—the Baby Potatoes with Aïoli being a particular favorite. Aïoli, the garlic mayonnaise from Catalonia, is the recipe that you will turn to time and time again when serving tapas dishes! It is a tapa classic and appears on every tapas menu. While we're on the subject, it can be written as one word as it is here or sometimes as ai-l-oli. Even the Spaniards themselves can't agree!

SERVES 6–8 AS PART
OF A TAPAS MEAL
2 oz/55 g serrano or prosciutto,
    pancetta, or rindless smoked
    lean bacon
4 oz/115 g chorizo sausage,
    outer casing removed
4 tbsp Spanish olive oil

1 onion, finely chopped
2 garlic cloves, finely chopped
splash of dry white wine
1 lb/450 g frozen fava beans, thawed,
    or about 3 lb/1.3 kg fresh fava
    beans in their pods, shelled to
    give 1 lb/450 g

1 tbsp chopped fresh mint or dill,
    plus extra to garnish
pinch of sugar
salt and pepper

Fava Beans with Serrano Ham

Both fresh and dried fava beans are highly regarded in Spain. In this recipe you can use fresh or, if more convenient, frozen fava beans, but if you choose the latter make sure that they are baby ones, as they are more tender. If you have time, you can remove the skins from the beans to reveal the soft, bright green bean inside, but it is a time-consuming task!

• Using a sharp knife, cut the ham, pancetta, or bacon into small strips. Cut the chorizo into ¾-inch/2-cm cubes. Heat the olive oil in a large, heavy-bottom skillet or ovenproof dish that has a lid. Add the onion and cook for 5 minutes, or until softened and starting to brown. If you are using pancetta or bacon, add it with the onion. Add the garlic and cook for 30 seconds.

• Pour the wine into the skillet, increase the heat, and let it bubble to evaporate the alcohol, then lower the heat. Add the fava beans, ham, if using, and the chorizo and cook for 1–2 minutes, stirring all the time to coat in the oil.

• Cover the skillet and let the beans simmer very gently in the oil, stirring from time to time, for 10–15 minutes, or until the beans are tender. It may be necessary to add a little water to the skillet during cooking, so keep an eye on it and add a splash if the beans appear to become too dry. Stir in the mint or dill and sugar. Season the dish with salt and pepper, but taste first as you may find that it does not need any salt.

• Transfer the fava beans to a large, warmed serving dish, several smaller ones, or individual plates and serve piping hot, garnished with chopped mint or dill.

MAKES 7–8
6½ oz/185 g canned or bottled whole
   pimientos del piquillo (charbroiled
   sweet red peppers)
salt and pepper
fresh herb sprigs, to garnish

CURD CHEESE AND HERB FILLING
1 cup curd cheese
1 tsp lemon juice

1 garlic clove, crushed
4 tbsp chopped fresh flatleaf parsley
1 tbsp chopped fresh mint
1 tbsp chopped fresh oregano
salt and pepper

OR TUNA MAYONNAISE FILLING
7 oz/200 g canned tuna steak in olive
   oil, drained
5 tbsp mayonnaise

2 tsp lemon juice
2 tbsp chopped fresh flatleaf parsley
salt and pepper

OR GOAT CHEESE AND OLIVE FILLING
scant ⅓ cup pitted black olives,
   finely chopped
7 oz/200 g soft goat cheese
1 garlic clove, crushed
salt and pepper

Stuffed Pimientos

Make sure that you buy whole bell peppers, not sliced. Pimiento is simply the Spanish word for pepper, but outside Spain the word is used to refer to red bell peppers that are cooked, peeled, and sold in jars or cans. If you can't find pimientos del piquillo, look for a jar of peppadew peppers from South Africa. This recipe will fill about 36 peppadew peppers.

• There is a choice of fillings provided in this recipe—the final decision is yours. Lift the peppers from the jar, reserving the oil for later.
• To make the Curd Cheese and Herb Filling, put the curd cheese in a bowl and add the lemon juice, garlic, parsley, mint, and oregano. Mix well together. Season to taste with salt and pepper.
• To make the Tuna and Mayonnaise Filling, put the tuna in a bowl and add the mayonnaise, lemon juice, and parsley. Add 1 tablespoon of the reserved oil from the jar of pimientos and mix well. Season to taste with salt and pepper.
• To make the Goat Cheese and Olive Filling, put the olives in a bowl, and add the goat cheese, garlic, and 1 tablespoon of the reserved oil from the jar of pimientos. Mix well together. Season to taste with salt and pepper.
• Using a teaspoon, heap the filling of your choice into each pimiento. Put in the refrigerator and let chill for at least 2 hours until firm.
• To serve the pimientos, arrange them on a serving plate and, if necessary, wipe with paper towels to remove any of the filling that has spread over the skins. Garnish with herb sprigs.

SERVES 8 AS PART
OF A TAPAS MEAL
2 tbsp Spanish olive oil
scant 1/3 cup pine nuts
1/2–1 tsp paprika

1 lb/450 g green beans
1 small onion, finely chopped
1 garlic clove, finely chopped
salt and pepper
juice of 1/2 lemon

Green Beans with Pine Nuts

As a variation to the pine nuts, you could use slivered or blanched almonds, which should be sliced into thin strips before cooking. They are equally delicious—it is simply a matter of personal preference.

• Heat the oil in a large, heavy-bottom skillet, add the pine nuts and cook for about 1 minute, stirring all the time and shaking the skillet, until light golden brown. Using a slotted spoon, remove the pine nuts from the skillet, drain well on paper towels, then transfer to a bowl. Set aside the oil in the skillet for later. Add the paprika, according to taste, to the pine nuts, stir together until coated, and then set aside.

• Trim the green beans and remove any strings if necessary. Put the beans in a pan, pour over boiling water, return to a boil, and cook for 5 minutes, or until tender but still firm. Drain well in a strainer.

• Reheat the oil in the skillet, add the onion and cook for 5–10 minutes, or until softened and starting to brown. Add the garlic and cook for an additional 30 seconds.

• Add the beans to the skillet and cook for 2–3 minutes, tossing together with the onion until heated through. Season the beans to taste with salt and pepper.

• Turn the contents of the skillet into a warmed serving dish, sprinkle over the lemon juice, and toss together. Sprinkle over the golden pine nuts and serve hot.

SERVES 8 AS PART
OF A TAPAS MEAL

3 red bell peppers

3 yellow bell peppers

5 tbsp Spanish extra virgin olive oil

2 tbsp dry sherry vinegar or
lemon juice

2 garlic cloves, crushed

pinch of sugar

salt and pepper

1 tbsp capers

8 small black Spanish olives

2 tbsp chopped fresh marjoram,
plus extra sprigs to garnish

Roasted Bell Pepper Salad

Although called roasted bell peppers, the bell peppers for this recipe are more usually broiled than roasted in an oven. You can also spear them on a fork and hold them over a gas flame, or roast them on a barbecue. Red and yellow bell peppers have been used here, but you can also use green ones or a mixture of colours.

• Preheat the broiler. Place the bell peppers on a wire rack or broiler pan and cook under a hot broiler for 10 minutes, until their skins have blackened and blistered, turning them frequently.
• Remove the roasted bell peppers from the heat, put them in a bowl, and immediately cover tightly with a clean, damp dish towel. Alternatively, you can put the bell peppers in a plastic bag. You will find that the steam helps to soften the skins and makes it easier to remove them. Let the peppers stand for about 15 minutes, until they are cool enough to handle.
• Holding one bell pepper at a time over a clean bowl, use a sharp knife to make a small hole in the base and gently squeeze out the juices and reserve them. Still holding the bell pepper over the bowl, carefully peel off the blackened skin with your fingers or a knife and discard it. Cut the bell peppers in half and remove the stem, core, and seeds, then cut each bell pepper into neat thin strips. Arrange the bell pepper strips attractively on a serving dish.
• To the reserved pepper juices add the olive oil, sherry vinegar, garlic, sugar, and salt and pepper to taste. Whisk together until combined. Drizzle the dressing evenly over the salad.
• Sprinkle the capers, olives, and chopped marjoram over the salad, garnish with marjoram sprigs, and serve at room temperature.

MAKES 32

2 tbsp Spanish olive oil, plus extra
    for brushing and drizzling
1 onion, finely chopped
1 garlic clove, finely chopped
14 oz/400 g canned chopped
    tomatoes
scant 3 cups baby spinach leaves
salt and pepper
2 tbsp pine nuts

BREAD DOUGH

4 tbsp warm water
½ tsp active dry yeast
pinch of sugar
generous 1¼ cups white bread
    flour, plus extra for dusting
½ tsp salt

Spanish Spinach and Tomato Pizzas

One associates pizzas with Italy, but in fact these Spanish pizzas are very popular tapas dishes called coca. They were traditionally made from a simple dough of flour and water, but now either a bread or pastry base is used. The toppings can vary too and might include anchovies, bell peppers, ham, chorizo sausage, and olives, but seldom cheese.

• To make the bread dough, measure the water into a small bowl, sprinkle in the dry yeast and sugar, and let stand in a warm place for 10–15 minutes, or until frothy.

• Meanwhile, sift the flour and salt into a large bowl. Make a well in the center of the flour and pour in the yeast liquid, then mix together with a wooden spoon. Using your hands, work the mixture until it leaves the sides of the bowl clean.

• Turn the dough out onto a lightly floured counter and knead for 10 minutes, or until smooth and elastic and no longer sticky. Shape into a ball and put it in a clean bowl. Cover with a clean, damp dish towel and let stand in a warm place for 1 hour, or until it has risen and doubled in size.

• To make the topping, heat the olive oil in a large, heavy-bottom skillet. Add the onion and cook for 5 minutes, or until softened but not browned. Add the garlic and cook for an additional 30 seconds. Stir in the tomatoes and cook for 5 minutes, letting it bubble and stirring occasionally, until reduced to a thick mixture. Add the spinach leaves and cook, stirring, until they have wilted a little. Season the mixture to taste with salt and pepper.

• While the dough is rising, preheat the oven to 400°F/200°C. Brush several baking sheets with olive oil. Turn the dough out onto a lightly floured counter and knead well for 2–3 minutes to knock out the air bubbles. Roll out the dough very, very thinly and, using a 2½-inch/6-cm plain, round cutter, cut out 32 circles. Place on the prepared baking sheets.

• Spread each base with the spinach mixture to cover, then sprinkle the pine nuts over the top. Drizzle a little olive oil over each pizza. Bake in the oven for 10–15 minutes, or until the edges of the dough are golden brown. Serve the spinach and tomato pizzas hot.

SERVES 8 AS PART
OF A TAPAS MEAL
1 lb/450 g baby zucchini
3 tbsp all-purpose flour
1 tsp paprika
1 large egg
2 tbsp milk

corn oil, for pan-frying
coarse sea salt
dipping sauce such as Aïoli (see
     page 92), Fiery Tomato Salsa
     (see page 61) or the Pine Nut
     Sauce (see below)

PINE NUT SAUCE
generous ½ cup pine nuts
1 garlic clove, peeled
3 tbsp Spanish extra virgin olive oil
1 tbsp lemon juice
3 tbsp water
1 tbsp chopped fresh flatleaf parsley
salt and pepper

Zucchini Fritters with a Dipping Sauce

The exact same
treatment can be applied
to eggplants, while the
Pine Nut Sauce can be
made with almonds in the
same way too, if preferred.

• If you have chosen to serve the pine nut sauce with the zucchini fritters, then make this first. Put the pine nuts and garlic in a food processor and blend to form a purée. With the motor still running, gradually add the olive oil, lemon juice, and water to form a smooth sauce. Stir in the parsley and season to taste with salt and pepper. Turn into a serving bowl.

• To prepare the zucchini, cut them on the diagonal into thin slices about ¼ inch/5 mm thick. Put the flour and paprika in a plastic bag and mix together. Beat the egg and milk together in a large bowl.

• Add the zucchini slices to the flour mixture and toss well together until coated. Shake off the excess flour. Pour enough corn oil into a large, heavy-bottom skillet for a depth of about ½ inch/1 cm, and heat. Dip the zucchini slices, one at a time, into the egg mixture, then slip them into the hot oil. Cook the zucchini slices, in batches of a single layer so that they do not overcrowd the skillet, for 2 minutes, or until crisp and golden brown.

• Using a slotted spoon, remove the zucchini fritters from the skillet and drain on paper towels. Continue until all the zucchini slices have been cooked.

• Serve the zucchini fritters piping hot, lightly sprinkled with sea salt. Accompany with a bowl of your chosen dipping sauce.

MAKES 12

2 tbsp Spanish olive oil

6 slices serrano ham

12 asparagus spears

pepper

Aïoli (see page 92), to serve

Roasted Asparagus with Mountain Ham

The most popular Spanish ham is serrano, which means mountain ham, because it is cured in the mountains. It is then aged from several months to several years. If you are unable to obtain it, you could use Italian prosciutto instead.

• Preheat the oven to 400°F/200°C. Put half the olive oil in a roasting pan that will hold the asparagus spears in a single layer and swirl it round so that it covers the bottom. Cut each slice of serrano ham in half lengthwise.

• Trim the ends of the asparagus spears, then wrap a slice of ham round the stem end of each spear. Place the wrapped spears in the prepared roasting pan and lightly brush the ham and asparagus with the remaining olive oil. Season the spears with pepper.

• Roast the asparagus spears in the oven for 10 minutes, depending on the thickness of the asparagus, or until tender but still firm. Do not overcook the asparagus spears as it is important that they are still firm.

• Serve piping hot, accompanied by a bowl of Aïoli for dipping.

SERVES 8 AS PART
OF A TAPAS MEAL
2 eggs
1 lb/450 g baby new potatoes,
    quartered
4 oz/115 g fine green beans, cut into
    1-inch/ 2.5-cm lengths
1 cup frozen peas
4 oz/115 g carrots

7 oz/200 g canned tuna steak
    in olive oil, drained
2 tbsp lemon juice
8 tbsp mayonnaise
1 garlic clove, crushed
salt and pepper
4 small gherkins, sliced
8 pitted black olives, halved
1 tbsp capers

1 tbsp chopped fresh flatleaf parsley
1 tbsp chopped fresh dill, plus extra
    sprigs to garnish

Russian Salad

This is one of Spain's most popular and staple tapas bar dishes. The vegetables that it contains vary, but usually the basic salad consists of potatoes, carrots, and peas, and sometimes tuna, as in this recipe.

• Put the eggs in a pan, cover with cold water, and slowly bring to a boil. Immediately reduce the heat to very low, cover and let simmer gently for 10 minutes. As soon as the eggs are cooked, drain them and put under cold running water. By doing this quickly, you will prevent a black ring from forming round the egg yolk. Gently tap the eggs to crack the eggshells and leave them until cold.

• Meanwhile, put the potatoes in a large pan of cold, salted water and bring to a boil. Lower the heat and let simmer for 7 minutes, or until just tender. Add the beans and peas to the pan for the last 2 minutes of cooking. Drain well, splash under cold running water, then let the vegetables cool completely.

• Cut the carrots into julienne strips about 1 inch/2.5 cm in length. Flake the tuna into large chunks. When the potatoes, beans, and peas are cold, put them in a large bowl. Add the carrot strips and the flaked tuna and very gently toss the ingredients together. Transfer the vegetables and tuna to a salad bowl or large serving dish.

• In a pitcher, stir the lemon juice into the mayonnaise to thin it slightly, then stir in the garlic and season to taste with salt and pepper. Drizzle the mayonnaise dressing over the vegetables and tuna.

• Sprinkle the gherkins, olives, and capers into the salad and finally sprinkle over the parsley and dill. You can store the salad in the refrigerator but return to room temperature before serving. Just before serving, crack the shells of the eggs all over and remove them. Slice the eggs into wedges, add them to the salad, and garnish with dill sprigs.

SERVES 6–8 AS PART
OF A TAPAS MEAL
1 lb/450 g baby new potatoes
1 tbsp chopped fresh flatleaf parsley
salt

AÏOLI
1 large egg yolk, at room temperature
1 tbsp white wine vinegar
   or lemon juice
2 large garlic cloves, peeled
salt and pepper
5 tbsp Spanish extra virgin olive oil
5 tbsp corn oil

Baby Potatoes with Aïoli

The recipe given here for Aïoli contains raw egg and therefore should be avoided by infants, the elderly, pregnant women, convalescents, and anyone suffering from an illness. If any of these cases applies to you, use commercially made mayonnaise and add the crushed garlic to it.

• To make the Aïoli, put the egg yolk, vinegar, garlic, and salt and pepper to taste in the bowl of a food processor fitted with the metal blade and blend well together. With the motor still running, very slowly add the olive oil, then the corn oil, drop by drop at first, then, when it starts to thicken, in a slow, steady stream until the sauce is thick and smooth. Alternatively, mix in a bowl with a whisk.

• For this recipe, the Aïoli should be a little thin so that it coats the potatoes. To ensure this, quickly blend in 1 tablespoon water so that it forms the consistency of sauce.

• To prepare the potatoes, cut them in half or quarters to make bite-size pieces. If they are very small, you can leave them whole. Put the potatoes in a large pan of cold, salted water and bring to a boil. Lower the heat and let simmer for 7 minutes, or until just tender. Drain well, then turn out into a large bowl.

• While the potatoes are still warm, pour over the Aïoli sauce, and gently toss the potatoes in it. Adding the sauce to the potatoes while they are still warm will help them to absorb the garlic flavor. Let stand for about 20 minutes to allow the potatoes to marinate in the sauce.

• Transfer the potatoes with Aïoli to a warmed serving dish, sprinkle over the parsley and salt to taste, and serve warm. Alternatively, the Aïoli can be served separately, allowing diners to dip the potatoes themselves.

SERVES 6 AS PART
OF A TAPAS MEAL
3 tsp paprika
1 tsp ground cumin
¼–½ tsp cayenne pepper
½ tsp salt

1 lb/450 g small old potatoes, peeled
corn oil, for pan-frying
sprigs of fresh flatleaf parsley,
   to garnish
Aïoli (see page 92), to serve (optional)

Pan-Fried Potatoes with Piquant Paprika

A variation is to cook the potatoes as here, then spoon over the Fiery Tomato Salsa that accompanies the Cheese Puffs (see page 61), or serve this spicy salsa separately for dipping the potatoes in. This dish is then known as Patatas Bravas (Bold Potatoes).

• Put the paprika, cumin, cayenne pepper, and salt in a small bowl and mix well together. Set aside.
• Cut each potato into 8 thick wedges. Pour corn oil into a large, heavy-bottom skillet to a depth of about 1 inch/2.5 cm. Heat the oil, then add the potato wedges, preferably in a single layer, and cook gently for 10 minutes, or until golden brown all over, turning from time to time, Remove from the skillet with a slotted spoon and let drain on paper towels.
• Transfer the potato wedges to a large bowl and, while they are still hot, sprinkle with the paprika mixture, then gently toss them together to coat.
• Turn the potatoes into a large, warmed serving dish, several smaller ones, or individual plates and serve hot, garnished with parsley sprigs. Accompany with a bowl of Aïoli for dipping, if wished.

Index